Talking About

Divorce

Nicola Edwards

Chrysalis Education

U.S. publication copyright © 2003 Chrysalis Education.
International copyright reserved in all countries.
No part of this book may be reproduced in any
form without written permission from the publisher.

Distributed in the United States by
Smart Apple Media
1980 Lookout Drive
North Mankato, Minnesota 56003

Copyright © Chrysalis Books PLC 2003

ISBN 1-93233-305-3

The Library of Congress control number 2003102414

Editorial manager: Joyce Bentley
Senior editor: Sarah Nunn
Picture researchers: Terry Forshaw, Lois Charlton
Designer: Wladek Szechter
Editor: Kate Phelps
Consultant: Dr Ute Navidi, Head of Policy, ChildLine

Printed in China

The pictures used in this book do not show the actual people named in the text.

Foreword

Divorce—and the periods before and after separation—can be difficult enough for adults. Wrapped up in their own problems, often struggling with raw emotions, parents may not notice how sad and confused their children are by what's happening. And children may find it hard to talk to their parents, anxious not to burden them further with their worries.

Talking About Divorce helps adults to listen and children to ask questions and express their views about divorce and separation. Together, they can explore the reasons why parents may decide to go their separate ways and talk about everyone's feelings when they do. That children can go on loving both parents is one of the book's reassuring messages, as well as telling children that divorce is never their fault. Identifying someone who will listen—a trusted adult, a friend of their own age, or a helpline—means taking the first step towards finding help.

Informative and thought-provoking, the **Talking About** series tackles some disturbing aspects of contemporary society: divorce, domestic violence, racism, eating problems, and bullying. Adults often try to protect children from these problems or believe they will not understand. Taking children through a series of situations they can identify with—using words and images—also means offering alternative ways of resolving conflict. Each book shows that even very young children are not passive observers or victims. They want to make sense of their world and act to make life better for themselves, their families, and other children.

Ute Navidi, Head of Policy, ChildLine (a U.K. helpline for children in distress)

Contents

What is divorce?

Divorce is when two
people decide they can't
live together any more.

When Michael's
parents got divorced,
Michael felt angry
and very sad.

It can take a long time for people to feel happy again after a divorce in the family.

Today, many **marriages** end in divorce. People who aren't married can decide to **separate**, too. When parents split up, it is sad and confusing for everyone.

Why do people get divorced?

When people get married or set up home together, it's an exciting time. But sometimes things don't work out as people hope.

When parents divorce, they live apart. So their children have two homes instead of one.

Sometimes when parents argue, they forget that their children can hear them.

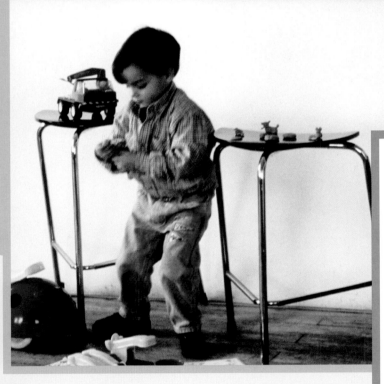

Just because couples argue, it doesn't have to mean they will split up.

There are lots of reasons why couples get divorced. They may grow apart and develop interests that they don't share. They may find that they want different things.

Feeling sad and worried

When a mom and dad are **arguing** at home, it can make their children very unhappy.

Rachel felt **lonely** and helpless because she couldn't stop her parents arguing.

David told his
aunt he was worried about
his parents arguing.

Parents can be so
wrapped up in their
problems, they can't
see how upset the
children are.

It's frightening for
children to hear the
people they love
shouting at each other.

If you are worried
about things at
home, tell someone
you **trust**.

The effect on the family

Children worry about their parents splitting up. Very young children often want someone to be with them all the time. They may have trouble sleeping, have nightmares, or wet the bed. Older children often feel very angry. They may take this anger out on others by **bullying** them.

Ginny comforted her brother when he had a nightmare about being left all alone.

John bullied his
brother because he was angry.
He didn't want his mom to leave home.

If your parents are splitting up,
you don't have to stop loving
both of them. They will always
be your mom and dad.

Spending time apart

Sometimes a couple decide to have a **trial separation**. This means that one of them moves away from home for a while.

Ravi's dad told him not to worry and that he would see him at the weekend.

Maria missed her mom and wanted her to come back home.

A trial separation gives both people the time and space to think things over and decide what they want to do. This is often a very worrying and upsetting time for children.

Is it my fault?

Children often feel that they are somehow to blame for their parents splitting up. They feel **guilty**. Sometimes they offer to be good if their parents will just get back together again.

Michelle's mom and dad told her she'd had nothing to do with them getting divorced.

14

But children are not **responsible** for how a mom and dad feel about each other.

Ruby felt sick when she thought about how her mom and dad were making each other unhappy.

A divorce is never the fault of a child.

Mom and dad forever

When a parent moves away from home, children can feel very scared and **confused**. They find it hard to believe their mom and dad really love them if they can leave them.

Lydia's mom told her that she would always love her.

Danny felt happy and
excited to be with his dad.

Your mom and dad
will always be your
mom and dad.

Children worry that their other parent
will leave, too. But when parents stop
being married, it doesn't mean they
stop loving their children.

What's happening?

When parents are splitting up, it can be hard for them to give their children all the care they need.

It helped Pui Chi when her parents explained how things would be different after their divorce.

Joseph talked to his dad
whenever he felt worried about anything.

Moms and dads are
often upset and worried
about the future for their
children after a divorce.
But it helps children
if their parents listen
to their views and
answer their questions.

It can help people
in a family to talk
about how they
are feeling.

Missing a parent

When parents get divorced it can mean that everyday life changes for everyone. The biggest change is that one home becomes two separate homes.

Jason's mom always sent him a present on his birthday.

Robin rang his dad to tell him he had won a prize in a competition.

Often after a divorce, the children live with one parent for most of the week. They see their other parent every weekend or every couple of weeks.

Children often miss their parent and wish they hadn't left home.

changes

Things can feel strange after a divorce. Children may have to move house and go to a different school. Their mom or dad may have a new **partner** who may have children of their own.

Ryan felt lonely at his new school. He missed his old friends.

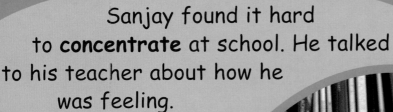

Sanjay found it hard
to **concentrate** at school. He talked
to his teacher about how he
was feeling.

Children may feel angry with their parents
for being responsible for these changes.
At home, there may be less money to
spend on food, clothes, or days out.

Time together, time apart

When children see their other parent on the weekend, it gives them a chance to spend time together.

Dan's dad moved in with his new partner and her daughter, Tara. Dan liked seeing his dad and playing with Tara.

Robert felt sad because he didn't see his mom much any more and he missed her.

Don't feel bad about loving your mom and dad equally.

When it's time to say goodbye at the end of a visit, it can be very upsetting for everyone. Children sometimes feel they are being **disloyal** to one parent if they enjoy spending time with the other.

You're not alone

Children whose parents are divorcing can feel unhappy when they see that their friends' parents are still together.

Henry's dad had a new partner but Henry still hoped his mom would come home.

Carly talked to her friend Jo about her parents' divorce. Jo's mom and dad had always lived apart and she was happy spending time with each of them.

Keeping worries bottled up inside doesn't make them go away. Sharing them can help.

But there are children in every school who have been through a divorce in the family. It can help to talk to each other about how it feels. Talking to brothers or sisters—or other relatives or family friends—can help, too.

Feeling happy again

There's no quick and easy way to feel happy again after a divorce. But parents who were sad together can become happier by living apart.

Liam's dad married again. Now Liam has a baby sister.

At first, Jane and Ed weren't sure about their mom's new partner. When they got to know him, they liked him a lot better.

It's easier for children to cope with divorce if they know their parents will always love them. Talking about what is happening and how everyone is feeling helps a lot, too.

Words to remember

arguing Having a disagreement.

bullying Hurting someone or making them feel sad.

concentrate To give something your full attention.

confused Feeling uncertain and mixed-up.

disloyal Not being true to someone or taking sides against them.

guilty Feeling as if you have done something you shouldn't.

lonely Feeling sad, as if you have no friends.

marriage When two people sign a paper during a ceremony and then live together as husband and wife.

partner Someone who is one half of a couple.

responsible Feeling that something is up to you.

separate To live apart.

trial separation To live apart for a while. After a trial separation, some couples decide to live together again and others decide to get divorced.

trust Feeling that someone won't let you down.

Organizations, helplines, and websites

Divorce Central
Gives information, including U.S. laws state-by-state and other legal points. Frequently asked questions are answered. An online Complete Parenting Handbook gives an A-Z guide to parenting children affected by divorce (helping children deal with grief, handling visits, single parenting...).
www.divorcecentral.com/

Divorceinfo.com
Gives information on a wide range of issues, from money to children. U.S. laws given state-by-state. Section on children offers advice on helping children through divorce, depresssion in children after divorce, dealing with anxiety etc.
www.divorceinfo.com

Divorce Magazine
Website with useful articles on a wide range of subjects and problems, such as how to help your kids, single parenting, father's rights, mother's rights, etc.
www.divorcemag.com

The Divorce Support Page
Explains issues, laws, resources available, child support and custody. Links to more sites.
www.divorcesupport.com

Kids' Turn
A non-profit organization helping kids and parents through divorce. Website includes questions and answers about divorce for kids, artwork by kids exploring feelings, activities to help kids understand divorce, book list to help kids learn more.
www.kidsturn.org/

Samaritans of Boston
Trained volunteers run a 24-hour helpline for anyone in distress:
617-247-0220

The publishers would like to point out that they are not responsible for the content of any of the websites featured on this page.

Index